Singing In The Wilderness

A Play

David Campton

Samuel French – London
New York – Sydney – Toronto – Hollywood

ISBN 0 573 12233 4

Please see page iv for further copyright information

CHARACTERS

Cobweb	Who finds herself, like it or not, the leader of this small band of fairies
Moth	A rather overweight pessimist
Mustard Seed	A not-too-bright optimist
Ecologist	A single-minded enthusiast
Folklorist	A cautious academic
Peaseblossom	Another fairy
Tinkerbell	A comparatively new fairy—is not seen, but whose conversation sounds like a bell tinkling

Time—the present

SINGING IN THE WILDERNESS

A clearing in a wood. It is night and a full moon is shining

A number of trees and bushes are suggested but only a small grass bank and three large bushes; L, C and R need be used. There are assorted plants and fungi growing

Throughout the play gentle woodland sounds can be heard

As the CURTAIN *rises we hear the tiny tinkle of a bell. The tinkle leaps from bush to bush and after being heard briefly in the distance, it is gone. After a slight pause Cobweb calls*

Cobweb (*off*) Tinkerbell ... ? Tinkerbell.

There is no reply as Cobweb and Moth enter, their fairy finery very bedraggled. Moth leans on the arm of Cobweb, who breathes heavily under the extra weight

Tinkerbell ... ! Idiot fairy. Always flying on ahead. What's the point when she only has to fly back?
Moth (*lugubriously*) Flying comes easy enough for those with workable wings. But when your wings are full of holes ...
Cobweb Moth been at them?
Moth (*halting*) I didn't laugh when you first made that joke, Cobweb, and it gets less funny every time you repeat it. You know as well as I do, it was acid rain.
Cobweb Don't be such a grizzle, Moth. Think yourself lucky you've still got a good pair of legs.
Moth These legs were never designed for long-distance walking.
Cobweb Only a few steps more.
Moth After all these miles, I've no more steps left in me.
Cobweb Look ahead. I spy a bank.
Moth (*eagerly*) Where wild thyme blows? With sweet musk roses and with eglantine?

They move forward

Cobweb Some hope in this day and age. At least you can take the weight off *your* feet and *my* arm. Here. Lower yourself.

Cobweb helps Moth to be seated

Moth Gently.

Cobweb I still say there must be something wrong with a fairy your shape. Even with wings in tip-top condition, I wouldn't expect them to lift you now.

Moth Blame the junk food. Picnickers with nothing but cola and crisps. Where has all the decent food gone?

Cobweb (*looking around*) Where has Mustard Seed gone?

Moth She stopped behind a bush.

Cobweb Again? (*She calls*) Mustard Seed!

Moth Must have been something she ate, too.

Cobweb Who ever heard of a fairy being sick?

Moth Mustard Seed can't help it.

Cobweb We can't risk becoming separated. Not after becoming separated from the others—Puck, Peaseblossom and the Changeling Boy.

Moth Why call him Boy? He must be three hundred years old if he's a day. He'd never have lasted so long if he hadn't been with us.

Cobweb But he isn't with us. Where is he? Where are they all? (*She calls furiously*) Mustard Seed! (*The effort of shouting brings on a fit of coughing*)

Moth Save your breath, Cobweb. You may need it.

Cobweb (*recovering slightly*) Dratted fumes! Percolate everywhere.

Moth We're not near a motorway, are we?

Cobweb Wherever we are, we're always near some belching exhaust. (*She raises her voice*) A murrain seize all internal combustion engines! (*This brings on another fit of coughing*)

Cobweb sits next to Moth on the bank

Moth Motor cars aren't subject to murrain. It's an infectious disease affecting cattle.

Cobweb tries to interrupt, but is still having difficulty with her chest

(*Gloomily*) I've never heard of a motor car with a murrain. Or even a tractor with the staggers, more's the pity.

Cobweb (*calling with difficulty*) Mustard ... Mus—— Oh, there
you are.

Mustard Seed enters with assumed brightness

Mustard Seed I really feel much better now.

Cobweb I advised you not to go after that nectar.

Mustard Seed But nectar is traditional fairy food. Nectar is full of
natural goodness.

Cobweb Not from a field that's just been sprayed.

Mustard Seed Fields were never sprayed in my young days.

Cobweb Your young days are long since past, Mustard Seed.

Moth *All* our young days are long since past.

Mustard Seed I can remember when we were Titania's favour-
ites—waiting on the Queen of Fairyland.

Cobweb Usually waiting for her to give the King something to
chew on before coming to dinner.

Mustard Seed Oh, those banquets! Nuts and honey.

Moth Curds and cream with heartsease and rose petals. And on
state occasions, a dormouse roasted whole.

Cobweb Are you trying to make her sick again?

Moth In those days we drank nothing but fresh morning dew.

Mustard Seed In those days our dresses were sewn from butterfly
wings.

Moth In those days I could dance on a moonbeam.

Cobweb These days you couldn't dance on a concrete beam. Stop
it, will you?

Mustard Seed Stop what?

Cobweb This mooning and glooming.

Moth Who's glooming? We're remembering.

Cobweb That's even worse.

Mustard Seed We were so gay in those days—when gay meant
gay. Puck, now. I never thought I'd say so, but I miss the little
wretch. At least he could make us laugh.

Moth Being a fairy's no fun any more.

Cobweb No more of that. We ought to be counting blessings.

Moth What blessings? My feet hurt.

Mustard Seed I suppose, looked at the right way, there's a
blessing. We shan't have to walk any further. We can rest here.
This is the first wood we've found for so long.

Moth Call this a wood? A straggle of trees between fields.

Mustard Seed We shan't find a better spot in this part of the world. Not since the hedgerows were grubbed up and the woodlands chopped down.

Moth I'm told there are pine forests in the north.

Cobweb Very monotonous—pine forests.

Moth Pine essence might improve your chest, Cobweb.

Cobweb Anyway, we're not in the north and you can't walk that far. So my chest will have to take its chance with what gets into it here. At least we have the bare necessities. Shelter of a sort. Oak and bramble.

Mustard Seed Come autumn there'll be blackberries and acorns here.

Cobweb We shan't. (*Her sharp retort brings on a bout of coughing*)

Mustard Seed Coltsfoot.

Cobweb (*wheezing*) Eh?

Mustard Seed I said "coltsfoot".

Cobweb Why?

Mustard Seed Coltsfoot is a specific against congestion.

Cobweb An interesting observation, but at this point in time, quite useless. Can you see any coltsfoot growing here?

Mustard Seed There.

Cobweb Where?

Mustard Seed Near the eyebright.

Cobweb jumps up and goes to investigate the plants

Cobweb Not coltsfoot! I thought selective weed-killers had done away with it all. The way they finished off the oxlips.

Mustard Seed Like those? The little spotted things *are* oxlips, aren't they?

Cobweb Coltsfoot and oxlips together? You'll be seeing musk rose and eglantine next. (*She looks up, suddenly staggered*) Musk rose! Eglantine!

Moth Don't excite yourself. They're only plants. Like wild thyme.

Cobweb At least I can't see any wild thyme.

Moth Because you've just been sitting on it.

Cobweb kneels down to inspect the bank

Cobweb I don't believe this.

Mustard Seed That's hardly fair on the flowers. You know how upset we turn when people say they don't believe in fairies.

Cobweb All these—together.

Mustard Seed We're all together. Three of us—and Tinkerbell, when she comes to look for us.

Cobweb That's different. Why are they here in this wood?

Moth Why are we? Perhaps they couldn't find a better place to settle in either.

Cobweb Is it a trick of the full moon? Or could some magic be at work?

Moth If there's any magic about, it won't be ours. The last spell I tried to weave had more holes in it than my wings. I can't even make this blister disappear.

Cobweb I begin to mistrust . . .

Mustard Seed Your senses, Cobweb? Not even moonlight could have me imagining the scent of woodbine. (*She sniffs*) Oh, yes.

Cobweb If I were a mouse I'd be sniffing cheese. Get up, Moth.

Moth Get up?

Cobweb We're moving on.

Moth Oh, no!

Cobweb Now. . . . Now.

Mustard Seed We can't go yet. Tinkerbell won't know where to find us.

Cobweb Then she must look until she does.

Moth The more I see of this place, the better I like it. Aren't these ladysmocks?

Mustard Seed These are mushrooms. (*She picks some and eats them*) We can't let them go to waste.

Cobweb My thumbs are pricking.

Moth Probably rheumatism. This wood may be cramped, but it *is* convenient. So right for us fairies.

Mustard Seed Such an inviting carpet of moss. It might have been specially laid. Oh, this is all too good to be true.

Cobweb It's true, all right, but I doubt if it's good.

Moth What are you afraid of, Cobweb?

Cobweb Remember Peaseblossom.

Moth We don't talk about Peaseblossom.

Mustard Seed We don't know what happened to Peaseblossom.

Cobweb Exactly.

Mustard Seed She wandered away and never came back.

Cobweb Why doesn't Tinkerbell come back?

Mustard Seed She will when she's ready.

Moth And we'll still be here. Sore feet and all. I must say mine feel better already. Perhaps this place is doing that. (*To Cobweb*) You're not coughing so badly now, and Mustard Seed hasn't been sick for at least ten minutes—even though she is stuffing herself with toadstools.

Mustard Seed Not toadstools. Chanterelles and quite delicious. Try some, Cobweb.

Cobweb No thank you. What *is* this place?

Mustard Seed You've heard of a bird sanctuary. Perhaps this is a fairy sanctuary.

Cobweb I don't trust it.

Moth You can do as you please. But I for one am not tramping over more miles of fields only to sleep in a ditch with a cola can for a pillow.

Mustard Seed We may never find so much good food in one place again. We can't leave it unpicked.

Cobweb Would you risk your neck for a handful of edible fungi?

Mustard Seed What risk?

Cobweb Ah.

Moth That's no answer.

Cobweb It will have to do until I can think of a better.

There is a distant tiny tinkle

  Tinkerbell! Here we are. Tinkerbell, here.

There is a tinkle, this time much closer

  Where have you been?

There is a tinkle

  What?

There is a tinkle

  How?

There is a tinkle

  Who?

There is a tinkle

  When?

There is a tinkle

So what did you do then?

The tinkle goes from bush to bush

Cobweb tries to follow the tinkle

Tinkerbell ... Tinker ... Tink ...

Moth A conversation with Tinkerbell is all very well when you're in the mood for party games. At any other time it can drive you mad.

Cobweb Don't get so excited. Settle down and tell me.

There is a tinkle near Cobweb

Go on.

There is a tinkle

You didn't!

There is a tinkle

They didn't!

There is a tinkle

You didn't!

There is a tinkle

They didn't!

There is a tinkle

Moth Somebody must have been busy doing nothing.

There is a continuous tinkle

Cobweb I understand. I understand perfectly. Yes, yes, yes.

The tinkle stops

Moth What was all that about?
Cobweb Weren't you listening?
Moth I heard—but to me it sounded like an accident at a cycle race.

There is a furious tinkle

Cobweb Now you've upset her. She ran into humans.
Mustard Seed Not humans!

Cobweb Two of them. She says they're coming this way.
Mustard Seed Oh, no!

There is a tinkle

Cobweb Following her tinkle.
Moth Oh, why can't she switch it off?

The tinkle fades into the distance

Mustard Seed Humans are responsible for the disasters that almost wiped us out. What can we do?
Moth Run.
Cobweb You?
Mustard Seed Hide.
Cobweb Where?
Moth How?
Mustard Seed Magic? A spell for invisibility.
Cobweb No time to weave one.
Moth And it's sure not to work.

The tinkle approaches rapidly

Mustard Seed There's no harm in trying.
Cobweb Tinkerbell says they're nearly here.
Moth Quick. Help me up!

Mustard Seed does a little dance in a circle with strange hand movements as Cobweb takes Moth's arm

Cobweb Heave! You ought to try a spell for losing weight.
Moth I have—but it only works with a calorie-controlled diet.

Cobweb heaves Moth to her feet

Cobweb What are you up to, Mustard Seed?
Mustard Seed Just a simple pattern—sort of knit one, purl one— for a quick fairy ring.
Cobweb Are you relying on that for safety?
Moth I'd rather trust the bushes.
Cobweb To the bushes then.

There is a continuous tinkle

Cobweb and Moth take cover behind separate bushes. Mustard Seed continues to weave her spell

Mustard Seed Grow bushes grow
                    And cover us so
                    Leaves and shoots hide us
                    Before eyes have spied us.
                    Let humans not see
                    Fairy folk such as we.
                    Hemlock and ivy——

Cobweb (*coming from behind her bush*) Mustard Seed!

Mustard Seed I'm not finished yet.

Cobweb You will be if you're caught. And Tinkerbell, stop telling everybody where we are.

The tinkle stops

Mustard Seed If loose ends aren't properly tied, the whole thing could come unwound.

Cobweb Your spells usually do.

There is a furious tinkle

    Whoops! (*She bolts behind her bush*)

Mustard Seed, after a frantic look round, hides behind another bush

Moth (*from behind her bush*) Is this bush big enough to hide me? Cobweb, where are you? I don't want to be left alone. Remember Peaseblossom.

Cobweb takes a step towards Moth's bush

There is a warning tinkle

Cobweb retreats quickly

The notes of a pipe or recorder can be heard in the distance

Mustard Seed (*appearing over her bush*) I don't feel well.

Moth (*appearing over her bush*) It's the excitement.

Cobweb (*appearing over her bush*) It's all those mushrooms.

Mustard Seed Only a few.

Cobweb Are you sure they were eatable?

Mustard Seed I ate them, didn't I?

Moth You should have concocted a spell against diarrhoea and sickness.

Cobweb Hush!

The notes of the pipe are heard very near

The fairies duck down behind their bushes

> *The Ecologist, an enthusiast from whom ideas and words are constantly bursting, and whose clothes seem to have been slung on at the last minute, hurries in on tip-toe. He carries a pipe or recorder*

Ecologist Is anyone there?

> *The Folklorist enters, a vaguely academic person, carrying a large butterfly net as though not quite sure why*

Folklorist What are we doing here? Following echoes?

Ecologist It sounded like a bell—and there are no bell birds in this hemisphere.

Folklorist I was perfectly happy at home with a cup of cocoa and Grimms' *Household Tales*.

Ecologist Listen.

Folklorist Why here? Why now? Why at all?

Ecologist There must have been something to follow, because we followed it.

Folklorist Nothing out of the ordinary. No witches or werewolves. Just birds or bats or badgers. Ordinary sights. Ordinary sounds.

Ecologist Only to ordinary souls. (*He plays a few notes on the pipe*)

Mustard Seed peeps over the bush

Folklorist I feel such a fool, waving this about. I'm glad nobody can see me.

Ecologist Don't be too sure. Eyes are everywhere.

Mustard Seed bobs down again

Folklorist Birds or bats. Thank heavens *they're* not going to ask what I'm doing at midnight with a butterfly net. So I don't have to answer "Trying to catch a fairy". That's enough to get anybody put away.

Ecologist But you're a folklorist. Fairies are your business. You are always writing about them. You lecture about them. You earn your living from them.

Folklorist That doesn't mean I have to believe in them.

Ecologist If you were a surgeon, would you confess to not believing in appendixes and hernias?

Folklorist Surgeons see appendixes every day. Hernias, too, for all I know. Who ever saw a fairy?

Ecologist Who *caught* a fairy and let it go?

Folklorist I didn't know it *was* a fairy at the time. I still don't know. It might have been a moth.

Ecologist (*excited*) A moth? Moth? (*Shouting derisively*) Moth!

Moth pops up from behind her bush

Moth Yes?

Ecologist (*explosively*) Hah!

Moth Oh!

Moth pops down again

Folklorist (*swinging round*) Ah!

Ecologist What?

Folklorist I thought. ... No. (*He turns back*) You were saying?

Ecologist A moth with wings this size? (*He opens his arms wide*) Shining?

Folklorist You weren't there.

Ecologist You told me all about it.

Folklorist My mistake.

Ecologist You know how I feel about endangered species.

Folklorist At that time you were busy saving the whale. Whales were no problem. You never dragged me out in the middle of the night with a net and a penny whistle to catch a whale.

Ecologist If fairies exist, they need to be protected.

Folklorist Ah. Now *you're* saying "if".

Ecologist I'm convinced. Others aren't. And they won't rally round until they are. Who'd give a brass farthing to save the whale if there were no whales left at all? It's no different with fairies. We must be able to say "Look—I told you so". Then funds will roll in. For more fairy parks like this. (*He prowls around the glade, looking for clues*)

Folklorist Who says they're here? Tonight.

Ecologist They've *been* here. I'm positive. I can almost smell them.

Cobweb pops up from behind her bush indignantly

Cobweb Really!

As the Folklorist's head jerks round, Cobweb pops down again

Ecologist (*who has not noticed Cobweb*) Lured by the flowers. Bushes bring the butterflies. You speculated on the same principle applying to fairies.

Folklorist I'd rather not be reminded.

Ecologist At the time you were fired with enthusiasm—pulling out armfulls of books from your shelves. Everything from *The Golden Bough* to Enid Blyton.

Folklorist Temporary insanity.

Ecologist You even helped me to plant this copse with wild-flowers. "Create the conditions and colonists will crowd in", you said.

Folklorist Who in their right minds would spend money and energy on folly like that?

Ecologist You did. Because you saw the thing you nearly caught.

Folklorist It might have been no more than a midsummer night's dream.

Ecologist Would anyone go to the trouble of transplanting an entire hawthorn hedge on account of a dream? You believed then.

Folklorist Oh, very well. If I say I believe now, can I go home to bed?

Ecologist If you still believe, you'll follow the trail with me. (*He drops to his hands and knees*) H'm.

Folklorist (*wearily*) What now?

Ecologist Examine this.

Folklorist I've seen it.

Ecologist Well?

Folklorist So what?

Ecologist As a student of natural sciences I could give a dissertation on non-edible fungi ... You folklorists have another name.

Folklorist I'm not saying another word.

Ecologist Not even—fairy ring?

Cobweb pops up from behind her bush

Cobweb Fairy ring?

Mustard Seed pops up from behind her bush

Mustard Seed I did it! I wove a spell.

Moth pops up from behind her bush

Moth But what spell?
Ecologist (*hearing something*) Ah!

As the Ecologist swings round, all the fairies pop down behind their bushes again. The Folklorist pretends nothing has happened

Folklorist I didn't notice a thing.
Ecologist They're here.
Folklorist Really?
Ecologist (*calling*) You can come out. Wherever you are. We're harmless.
Folklorist Perhaps they don't understand English.
Ecologist They're English fairies, aren't they? We must establish communication. (*He plays a few notes on his pipe*)
Folklorist Does that mean you'll be spending the rest of the night here?
Ecologist The rest of the year if necessary. Now I've run them to earth, I can't let them go.
Folklorist You talk as though they're your personal property.
Ecologist In the field of research, it's finders keepers.
Folklorist Then I hope They don't understand what you're saying.
Ecologist They could be anywhere. Search for them. Among the cowslips. Up a tree. Behind those bushes ...
Mustard Seed (*from behind her bush*) Ooooh!
Moth (*from behind her bush*) Don't be sick now, Mustard Seed.
Cobweb (*from behind her bush*) Hold your breath and count to a hundred.
Ecologist There. Didn't you hear?
Folklorist Rustling and twittering.
Ecologist Fairy talk.
Folklorist Huh.
Ecologist Follow me.
Folklorist Behind the bushes?
Ecologist Gently with that butterfly net. Don't frighten them.

The Ecologist tiptoes behind the bushes, followed by the Folklorist. As they do so, the Fairies tiptoe round to the front

Moth Can they see us?
Cobweb Not as long as we keep the bushes between them and us.
Moth I mean—did Mustard Seed really weave a spell to make us invisible?

Cobweb I can still see you.

Mustard Seed But can *They*?

Cobweb There's one way to check. Let them have a look at you.

Moth No, thank you.

Ecologist (*from behind the bush*) There's nothing to be afraid of. We want to help. Just show yourselves.

The fairies freeze

Folklorist (*from behind the bush*) No sign here.

Ecologist (*from behind the bush*) But I heard them, I tell you. Chatter, chatter, chatter. Like so many starlings.

Cobweb (*in a furious whisper*) More insults.

Moth (*whispering back*) In the good old days we'd have wished them bad luck.

Mustard Seed (*whispering*) No need, Humans *are* bad luck.

Ecologist (*as though talking to birds*) Come, come, come. Pretty, pretty, pretty.

Mustard Seed Pretty?

Cobweb Flattery now.

Folklorist (*from behind the bush*) There's nothing here. Not even a bell.

Cobweb A bell?

Ecologist (*from behind the bush*) You said you couldn't hear it.

Folklorist (*from behind the bush*) Now you know why. There isn't one.

Ecologist (*from behind the bush*) There was.

Cobweb Tinkerbell! She led them here. They'll follow her anywhere.

Mustard Seed Will they?

Cobweb She'll lead them away. (*She calls*) Tinkerbell!

Moth Hush. Don't shout.

Ecologist (*from behind the bush*) Hear that?

Moth They're coming back.

The fairies return behind their bushes just in time to avoid the Ecologist and Folklorist coming back round to the front

Ecologist You didn't catch a glimpse out of the corner of your eye?

Folklorist I wasn't looking out of the corner of my eye.

Cobweb (*calling from behind the bush*) Oh, Tinkerbell! Please ...

Ecologist Hark!

Cobweb (*from behind her bush*) Tink. Tink! Tink!!

Ecologist Ah!

Moth (*from behind her bush*) Oh, shut up, Cobweb.

Ecologist Very well. Visible or invisible, I'll talk to you.

Cobweb (*from behind her bush*) Where have you gone, Tink?

Ecologist (*as though addressing a public meeting*) One, two or many of you gathered here tonight, I exhort you to accept that I am acting only in your vital interests. Our countryside is not what it was. Pesticides, herbicides, urban development, industrial expansion and even stubble burning have all wreaked havoc. However, my companion and I have created a modest environment calculated to maintain the quality of life as delineated by the most reliable authorities—to wit the songs and stories of our ancestors.

Folklorist Why not come straight to the point? Fairies need somewhere to live. Here it is.

Ecologist I couldn't have expressed myself better. What does a fairy need? Here it is. Old English trees—none of your Scandinavian coniferous imports, but oak and ash and bonny ivy tree. Mossy banks by running brooks, well-stocked with stickleback and tiddlers, marsh marigolds and water cress. For you we have put the clock back three hundred years. Even to spotted snakes with double tongues—and they took some establishing, I can tell you. Slippery customers, snakes. You will be safe here. As long as you don't stray from these woods again. But then, why should you? There is everything here to keep you. I mean—to keep you happy.

Folklorist It's a very little wood.

Ecologist It's the biggest we could get at the price. And it contains everything a fairy needs.

Folklorist Everything?

Ecologist Nectar without artificial additives, colouring or preservatives.

Folklorist That isn't everything a fairy needs.

Ecologist Everything that I can think of.

Folklorist Except, perhaps, freedom.

Ecologist That's the first time you've mentioned freedom.

Folklorist It's the first time I've thought of it.

Ecologist Anyway, freedom's all very well in theory—until it proves lethal. Ask any rabbit that's just been nobbled by a hawk.

Cobweb (*from behind her bush*) How can we escape without being seen?

Moth (*from behind her bush*) Who wants to escape?

Cobweb (*from behind her bush*) Anyone in prison.

Folklorist Prison's prison, no matter how you look at it.

Ecologist Don't look at this as a prison. More as a museum. They may even enjoy it.

Folklorist Does a butterfly enjoy being pinned on a card?

Ecologist Fairies are different.

Folklorist Don't they mind being pinned on a card?

Ecologist We'll keep them safe and happy.

Folklorist Happy?

Ecologist Comfortable. Away from all that pollution. (*To the fairies*) Are you still listening, my dears?

Mustard Seed (*from behind her bush*) We're listening.

Cobweb (*from behind her bush*) Put your hands over your ears.

Ecologist Here you'll be guarded all the time. Against droughts, louts, frostbite and vandals. We can form an association. ROSPOF.

Folklorist ROSPOF?

Ecologist The Royal Society for the Protection of Fairies.

Mustard Seed (*from behind her bush*) Why did we ever think of them as hostile?

Ecologist Once we have established our legal claim.

Folklorist Our? Do you intend to keep them to yourself?

Ecologist In a way our fairies are everybody's fairies. We merely established the first reservation. But we shall need to keep a strict control over visitors.

Folklorist Visitors?

Ecologist No undesirables or coach parties. We might issue special licences for cameras and binoculars.

Folklorist (*with growing alarm*) You mean—they'll be on show?

Ecologist The curious are bound to come anyway—the way they crowd into safari parks. When did they last have the chance to observe a fairy in its natural state? We'd only make a small charge to cover expenses—maintaining pathways, hides, toilets and car parks.

Folklorist Car parks?

Cobweb (*from behind her bush*) Petrol fumes! (*She coughs*)

Folklorist (*sarcastically*) No hot-dog stands or hamburger concessions?

Ecologist Not at first. Profits aren't as important as honours. (*He is now launched on a pink cloud of speculation*) Honorary degrees. OBE, MBE, CBE—how high do the BEs go? There might even be a Nobel prize in time. Shared, of course. Between those who can be said to have shared the work.

Folklorist (*angrily*) Is that a temptation or a threat?

Ecologist You wouldn't refuse the prestige. Or the royalties on "I Found Fairyland".

Folklorist You are supposed to be an ecologist—not a showman.

Ecologist (*defensively*) Even an ecologist has a right to recognition.

Folklorist And you started out with such good intentions, didn't you?

Ecologist (*also becoming angry*) There is nothing wrong with my intentions. They haven't changed. We can't let fairies go the way of dodos.

Folklorist That might be best after all—for them and for you.

Ecologist I am going to save them. Single-handed if I must.

Folklorist (*striding away*) At a pound a head plus VAT?

Ecologist Where do you think you're going?

Folklorist Home.

Ecologist Where the only fairies are in books.

Folklorist Where they belong.

Ecologist If you go now, you won't share in the glory.

Folklorist It's all yours. (*He offers the Ecologist the butterfly net*) As Mrs Beeton might have said, "First catch your fairy".

Ecologist (*snatching the butterfly net*) I shall. Don't fret. I shall.

The Folklorist turns to go, pauses and turns back for a final shot

Folklorist Are they still about? Are you quite sure you're not talking to yourself?

The Folklorist exits

Ecologist (*shouting to the Folklorist as he goes*) So you're leaving them to me, are you? From now on they're all mine. Talking to myself? Of course I'm not. (*To the fairies*) You . . . you *are* still here.

Mustard Seed (*from behind her bush*) Yes.

Cobweb (*from behind her bush*) Mustard Seed! What are you thinking of?

Mustard Seed (*from behind her bush*) Mushrooms.

Ecologist Don't go. Where else will you find a haven like this?

Moth (*from behind her bush*) True.

Ecologist Without me, how long will it remain a refuge?

Cobweb (*from behind her bush*) You don't want to join that profiteer.

Ecologist Why aren't you co-operating?

Cobweb (*from behind her bush*) We are fairies, not freaks.

Ecologist Why don't you ring your little bell again?

Cobweb emerges from behind the bush

Cobweb If only Tinkerbell *were* here. Come back Tink. Come back.

Ecologist If only to show where you are.

Mustard Seed emerges from behind the bush to take Moth's hand

Mustard Seed We've been cold and hungry for so long.

Cobweb Can you imagine what Moth will look like once visitors start tossing buns to her?

Moth We don't want to keep walking for ever.

Cobweb Do you want to be fenced in for ever? Because once that one gets control over you——

Ecologist You . . .

The fairies cluster behind the middle bush

All our problems will be over once the public is persuaded to believe in you. With enough true believers we could extend these woods. Lay a carpet of bluebells. Create a setting for a fairy queen . . .

Cobweb (*from behind the bush*) At a pound a head, plus VAT?

Ecologist Just give me proof you're here. Come out. Come out, wherever you are.

Mustard Seed (*from behind the bush*) I'm coming.

Mustard Seed emerges from behind the bush

Cobweb (*from behind the bush; desperately*) Tinkerbell!

Ecologist Are you trying to talk to me?

Moth (*from behind the bush*) She said we're coming.

Moth emerges from behind the bush

Ecologist I can't hear you.
Moth ⎫
Mustard Seed ⎬ (*shouting together*) We're here!

There is a tinkle

Ecologist Yes. I heard that.
Cobweb (*from behind the bush; with great relief*) Tinkerbell!

There is a tinkle

The Ecologist turns in the direction where the tinkle is heard

Ecologist I still can't see you.
Moth You're not looking at us.
Cobweb (*from behind the bush*) Where have you been all this time?

There is a tinkle

Cobweb (*from behind the bush*) This is no laughing matter.
Ecologist This is all very well, but why don't you come out?
Mustard Seed We *are* out.
Ecologist There's no need to hide.
Moth Who's hiding?
Ecologist Seeing is believing.
Moth Then look this way.

The tinkle moves to the bush furthest away from the Ecologist

Cobweb Not that way, Tinkerbell!

Cobweb hurries from behind the bush towards the tinkle

The Ecologist turns to face the direction of the sound and faces the fairies—but sees nothing

Ecologist A few customers may pay up on trust, but an exhibition of invisible fairies could irritate the Office of Fair Trading.
Moth But we're ...
Mustard Seed Ooooh!
Moth What now?
Mustard Seed My spell. We did become invisible.
Moth I can see you.

There is a tinkle

Mustard Seed They can't.
Ecologist For goodness sake, reveal yourselves.

There is a tinkle

Ecologist I am a patient person. My patience is almost unlimited.

There is a tinkle

Ecologist But that limit has been reached.

There is a tinkle

Moth Did you include fern seed in your spell?
Mustard Seed I can't remember.
Moth Take it off.
Mustard Seed I can't.

There is a tinkle

Ecologist (*with mounting frustration*) I can tell where you are by
the tinkle. And when I catch you, there'll be no escaping again.

There is a tinkle

The Ecologist lunges with the net in the direction of the sound. The
fairies scatter

Ecologist Without me you're doomed, you fools. Doomed!
Cobweb Quickly, Tink. Through bog, through break, through
bush, through briar . . .
Mustard Seed That's Puck's game.
Cobweb Will serve.

The tinkle darts from bush to bush

The Ecologist follows the tinkle with his net

Ecologist I tell you nobody cares about you but me. Money is all
that matters. Speed means money. Pollution means money.
Contamination means money. Money makes monsters. How
long do you expect to last in a world where conservation is only
a word? Eh? Eh? (*He lunges with the net*) Ah. Ah. Ah!

The tinkle fades into the distance

The Ecologist exits following the tinkle

(*Off*) I won't have my triumph snatched away. I know a trick worth two. (*Fading in the distance*) We're in business whether you like it or not.

There is a slight pause while the fairies get their breath back

Mustard Seed Well, now ...
Moth Now what?

Ironic applause, from one pair of hands, can be heard approaching

Mustard Seed Who's that?

Peaseblossom enters, clapping, from the direction in which the Ecologist has disappeared

Peaseblossom What time is the next performance?
Cobweb Peaseblossom!
Peaseblossom Well met by moonlight, my dears.
Mustard Seed How did you find us?
Peaseblossom Tinkerbell led the way.
Cobweb What are you doing in these woods? So near to those humans.
Peaseblossom Can't you guess? I'm the one that got away. I remembered how to vanish just in time.
Mustard Seed Did you——?
Peaseblossom Do the same for you? Exactly.
Mustard Seed So it wasn't my spell after all.
Peaseblossom You raised a pretty ring of toadstools. Not everybody can do that.
Moth Well, now you can reverse the charm.
Peaseblossom I'm afraid I can't. I've forgotten how.
Cobweb Until you do, we'll remain invisible to humans.
Peaseblossom As far as I know. Does that matter so much?
Cobweb Not at all. In that case we might stay here.
Peaseblossom I wouldn't advise it. The mortals know we're here. They can be so devious, and we're such simple souls at heart.
Mustard Seed It seems such a pity to leave all this.
Peaseblossom It won't stay this way. The modern world is sure to bulldoze its way back. Not even fairies can reverse the clock.
Mustard Seed What can we do, then?
Peaseblossom Adapt.
Moth To acid rain?

Peaseblossom Even to acid rain.

Cobweb So we must start to walk again.

Peaseblossom Better be on our way.

Mustard Seed What about Tinkerbell?

Peaseblossom She'll catch up. She's a very new fairy. Less than a
hundred years old. So much more agile than we older ones.

Moth You don't recall a spell for warding off blisters, do you?

Peaseblossom Not off-hand.

Moth Pity.

Peaseblossom If one should come to mind, I'll let you know.
Though I found that singing kept my spirits up wonderfully.

Cobweb We could try that.

Peaseblossom All together, then. "Where the bee sucks, there suck
I ..."

Cobweb That's Ariel's song.

Peaseblossom Ariel won't mind, and we all know it.

*Peaseblossom starts to sing. Cobweb and Moth join in as they walk
away. Mustard Seed hangs back for a while*

Mustard Seed (*looking around*) There'll be berries here in the
autumn. And nuts. And.... Oh, well.... Perhaps we'll be back.

*Mustard Seed runs to catch up with the others, loudly joining in the
singing*

CURTAIN

FURNITURE AND PROPERTY LIST

On stage: Small grass bank
Three large bushes
Assorted plants and fungi including mushrooms

Off stage: Large butterfly net **(Folklorist)**

Personal: **Ecologist:** pipe or recorder

LIGHTING PLOT

Property fittings required: nil

To open: Full moonlight

No cues

EFFECTS PLOT